Alice IN THE COUNTRY OF Hearts

Volume 1
Scholastic Edition

Created by
QuinRose X Soumei Hoshino

HAMBURG // LONDON // LOS ANGELES // TOKYO

Alice in the Country of Hearts Volume 1 Scholastic Edition
Created by QuinRose X Soumei Hoshino

Translation - Beni Axia Conrad
English Adaptation - Lianne Sentar
Retouch and Lettering - Star Print Brokers
Production Artist - Rui Kyo
Graphic Designer - Al-Insan Lashley

Editor - Cindy Suzuki
Print Production Manager - Lucas Rivera
Managing Editor - Vy Nguyen
Senior Designer - Louis Csontos
Art Director - Al-Insan Lashley
Director of Sales and Manufacturing - Allyson De Simone
Associate Publisher - Marco F. Pavia
President and C.O.O. - John Parker
C.E.O. and Chief Creative Officer - Stu Levy

A TOKYOPOP® Manga

TOKYOPOP and are trademarks or registered trademarks of TOKYOPOP Inc.

TOKYOPOP Inc.
5900 Wilshire Blvd. Suite 2000
Los Angeles, CA 90036

E-mail: info@TOKYOPOP.com
Come visit us online at www.TOKYOPOP.com

ISBN: 978-1-4278-3146-0

First TOKYOPOP printing: July 2010
10 9 8 7 6 5 4 3 2 1
Printed in the USA

ハートの国のアリス
~Wonderful Wonder World~
1

C O N T E N T S

♥1 Welcome to Wonderland

AN OUT-SIDER?

SERI-OUSLY?!

WHAT A RUDE TART.

SHE TOTALLY BLEW YOU OFF, BLOOD.

I THINK THAT YOUNG LADY'S AN OUTSIDER, ELLIOT.

YEAH.

HUFF HUFF

HUFF

...MAYBE IT WAS WEIRD TO JUST RUN OUT OF THERE WITHOUT THINKING.

"ALICE..."

"YOU'RE WELCOME, SWEETHEART."

I HAVE TO CALM DOWN. IT'S NOT HIM... IT'S NOT...

HOW VERY... CURIOUS...

I SUPPOSE YOU'RE AN OUTSIDER, THEN.

OUT- SIDER?

THEN YOU... OH, CURSE IT ALL.

YES. FROM THIS GLASS THING.

I HAVE NO CHOICE. COME--I'LL EXPLAIN THINGS.

THAT'S RIGHT.

THE "PETER" YOU MENTIONED EARLIER. DO YOU MEAN PETER WHITE?

MY ROOM WAITS.

THAT BLASTED RABBIT!

Tch.

HE SMUGGLED YOU IN WITHOUT MY PER- MISSION.

YOU ARE AN *OUTSIDER*. YOU'RE NOT A RESIDENT OF THIS COUNTRY.

I AM JULIUS MONREY THE OWNER OF THIS CLOCK TOWER.

NOW, ALICE LIDDELL.

I KNOW THAT OUTSIDERS USUALLY COME HERE OF THEIR OWN VOLITION, BUT--

AND IT IS DANGEROUS FOR OUTSIDERS TO WALK AROUND THIS LAND IN IGNORANCE.

YES.

YOU DID MENTION THAT YOU WERE FORCED.

I'M TELLING YOU I DIDN'T--

I'M SURPRISED YOU'VE MET THEM AND STILL HAVE YOUR HEAD INTACT.

ELLIOT MARCH AND THE BLOODY TWINS...

...ARE DANGEROUS PEOPLE WHO ARE QUICK TO WIELD THEIR WEAPONS.

FROM WHAT YOU'VE TOLD ME...

...YOU WERE IN THE HATTER'S TERRITORY EARLIER.

A TRIANGULAR TUG-OF-WAR CAN DRAG ON FOR A LONG TIME.

SO IS THIS "WAR" THING WHY EVERYONE CARRIES WEAPONS?

IT'S AN UNPRODUCTIVE GAME.

THE BATTLE HAS NOTHING TO DO WITH OUTSIDERS, SO TAKE CARE NOT TO GET INVOLVED.

WELL, PARTIALLY.

BUT YOU'LL LEARN MORE ABOUT THAT LATER.

I WANT TO GO HOME.

I CAN GO ALONE IF SOMEONE JUST TELLS ME HOW.

LOOK, I APPRECIATE YOU EXPLAINING THIS STUFF.

BUT I DON'T *PLAN* TO GET INVOLVED--I DON'T EVEN WANT TO STAY.

WHAT? UH...

THEN WILL *YOU* TAKE ME?

UN-LIKELY.

NOT ALONE, AT ANY RATE.

"YOU CANNOT GO HOME ALONE."

IT'S A RULE OF THE GAME THAT YOU, AS AN OUTSIDER, PARTICIPATE IN.

IT'S NOT THAT SIMPLE.

♥2 On the way

THAT PETER GUY'S THE PRIME MINISTER OF HEART CASTLE?

THAT PLACE MUST BE RUN BY A GROUP OF PSYCHO-PATHS.

YOU'RE KIDDING, RIGHT? HE'S A PERV AND A... RABBIT!

ALL THE SAME, IT'S THE TRUTH.

[A]T LEAST NOW I KNOW WHERE HE IS.

....

I WANTED TO ASK HIM WHY HE DRAGGED ME HERE.

And kick him in the crotch, hopefully.

WERE YOU PLANNING TO GO SEE HIM?

[P]LEASE BE MINDFUL OF YOUR SAFETY.

...BUT I'LL BE DARNED IF I CAN'T WALK AROUND IN MY OWN DREAM.

IT MAY BE DANGER-OUS OUT THERE...

ANYWAY, ACE.

ARE YOU FINALLY HERE TO FACE THE HATTER?

SORRY ABOUT EARLIE GIRLIE. AN DON'T WORR I DON'T FEEL LIKE SHOOTING Y ANYMORE

CLUELESS.

NO. WHY?

BLOOD... HUH.

...PLUS, BLOOD WON'T LET ME.

WE'RE JUST HEADED FOR THE CASTLE.

THIS IS OUR TERRITORY AND THE ONLY THING PAST HERE IS THE MANSION.

SO OF

YOU'VE GOT THE DIRECTION SENSE OF A BLIND LEMMING!

HOW MANY TIMES DO I HAVE TO TELL YOU THAT?!

HUH?!

DID I GO THE WRONG WAY AGAIN?

THERE ISN'T! GET THAT THROUGH YOUR THICK SKULL!

BUT THERE'S A ROAD TO THE CASTLE PAST HERE--

HMM.

WAIT.

YOU'RE RIDICULOUS.

I'D LIKE NOTHING MORE THAN TO PUT A BULLET IN YOUR BRAIN, AND THE CUTE ACT IS ONLY MAKING ME MADDER.

THEN...THAT EXPLAINS WHY HE WAS WANDERING IN THE BUSHES!

Ha ha ha!

REALLY? I DON'T MEAN TO BE CUTE.

HONESTLY, GETTING LOST ISN'T SO BAD--IT ALWAYS LEADS ME TO NICE GUYS. LIKE YOU!

I'M GRATEFUL TO YOU, MAN. YOU LED ME OUT OF HERE LAST TIME TOO!

・・・・・・・

YOU DON'T SAY!

NOW LISTEN.

HEY!

DON'T GET LOST WHILE I'M TALKING TO YOU!

THE CASTLE IS IN THE **OPPOSITE DIRECTION** FROM THE WAY YOU WERE WALKING.

HA HA HA HA HA!

YOU HAVE A REAL PROBLEM, DINGBAT! GET HELP!

...THEY'RE SO LOUD.

YOU'RE STARING. IS THERE SOMETHING ON MY FACE?

HUH?

· · · · · · ·

AND I DARESAY I FELT YOU STARING AT ME EARLIER. GAWKING IS A LITTLE... NAUGHTY.

NO! I JUST...

BLUSH

I WAS SO SURPRISED THAT I RAN AWAY FROM YOU LAST TIME.

...THAT WAS RUDE.

Y-YOU LOOK A LOT LIKE SOMEONE I KNOW.

WELCOME HOME, SIR ACE!

IT'S GOOD TO BE BACK.

AND WELCOME, GUEST.

PETER'S USUALLY WITH THE QUEEN.

WE CAN TRY THE AUDIENCE CHAMBER.

MAYBE I'LL DO THAT, THANKS.

AH... IN SUCH A STATE, YOU WILL BE ASLEEP BEFORE YOU REACH THE CLOCK TOWER.

YOU MUST REST AT THE CASTLE, IF ONLY FOR NOW.

WHITE, SEE HER TO THE GUEST ROOMS.

YES, MAJESTY!

Huh?!

I DON'T NEED YOUR HELP!

AND STOP TOUCH-ING ME!

SLAP

YOU'RE NOT STEADY AT ALL!

TAKE MY ARM OR YOU'LL FALL.

フラ?!

GREAT.

· · · · · · ·

I'M STILL HERE...I'M STILL STUCK IN THIS PLACE.

I'M GOING BACK TO THE CLOCK TOWER.

I'VE BEEN OUT LONGER THAN I WANTED, AND JULIUS MIGHT BE WORRIED.

PLEASE, ALICE!

DON'T BE WITH HIM INSTEAD OF ME!

YOU CAN IGNORE HIM! I ENCOURAGE IT!

THAT'S SO CLOSE TO ADULTERY!

SHAKE SHAKE

MUST YOU LEAVE SO SOON?

YOU'VE JUST LEFT YOUR ROOM!

PLEASE DON'T LEAVE!

HE LOOKS LIKE A PUNK... AND A CAT.

THIS IS BORIS. HE'S OUR PAL.

BORIS LIVES IN THE AMUSEMENT PARK.

A PUNK CAT. FOR GOD'S SAKE.

WHAT'S UP, ALICE?

AMUSEMENT PARK?

AMUSEMENT PARK?

I DON'T THINK ANYONE CARES. I'M JUST A FREELOADER, AND THESE GUYS ARE HIRED GOONS.

Right?

Yeah.

I THOUGHT THE AMUSEMENT PARK AND THE HATTERS WERE FIGHTING OVER TERRITORIES.

THE OLD MAN AND THE HATTER DO HATE EACH OTHER'S GUTS, THOUGH.

AN' THERE WASN'T ANYTHIN' THAT SAID "YOU CAN'T BE FRIENDS WITH THE ENEMY" IN OUR CONTRACT.

IS IT OKAY FOR YOU GUYS TO HANG OUT?

...I THINK I'D LIKE TO SEE HIM FALL OFF THAT HORSE.

IF A PRINCE ON A WHITE HORSE ACTUALLY APPEARED IN FRONT OF ME...

BUT...

"IF YOU REALLY LOOKED AT ME WITH THAT HEAT..."

...IF HE WASN'T A PRINCE ON A WHITE HORSE TO BEGIN WITH...

...WHAT WOULD I WANT THEN?

♡4 Clock&Afterimage

IT'S RISEN AGAIN.

THE VIAL'S FILLING UP.

BUT THE MORE I TALK TO THE PEOPLE OF THIS PLACE, THE MORE THE BOTTLE FILLS UP AGAIN.

PETER FORCED ME TO DRINK THIS MEDICINE.

BUT I'M SURE I DIDN'T WANT A WORLD LIKE THAT.

"EVERYONE IN THIS WORLD IS GOING TO FALL IN LOVE WITH YOU."

HEY, ARE YOU ALL RIGHT?!

ARE YOU HURT?!

HANG ON--I'M GOING FOR HELP!

HE'S NOT DEAD, IS HE...?

HE'S NOT ANSWERING.

DID I SEE THOSE THINGS EARLIER?!

?!

YOU WEREN'T IN YOUR ROOM...I GUESS YOU WERE HERE.

JULIUS?

HM? OH.

IT'S YOU AGAIN.

I HAD SOME... BUSINESS.

YOU WERE QUITE LATE RETURNING HERE, YOU KNOW.

You were talking to yourself? Is your head okay?

NO ONE, REALLY. I'M ALONE HERE.

GLANCE GLANCE

WHO WERE YOU TALKING TO?

WELL, I WASN'T OUT HAVING *FUN*.

OH. SO I GUESS YOU *DID* WORRY.

I met a lot of people, though.

I GOT LOST, MIXED UP IN A FIGHT AND WITNESSED A GUN DEATH. IT WAS AWFUL.

HRM.

IF PEOPLE THINK I'VE ABANDONED AN OUTSIDER, MY REPUTATION COULD BE AT STAKE.

YOU SEEM TO KNOW A LOT ABOUT THEM, SO I THOUGHT YOU MIGHT KNOW SOMETHING.

I DON'T.

YOUR JOB IS TO FIX CLOCKS, RIGHT?

I DON'T BELIEVE YOU!

I THINK YOU'RE HIDING SOMETHING.

YOU REALLY DON'T KNOW ANYTHING?

Come on!

I SIMPLY DON'T HAVE ANYTHING TO TELL YOU.

WH...

DON'T BLOW ME OFF, OKAY?!

IT HAS NOTHING TO DO WITH AN OUTSIDER LIKE YOU.

YOU'LL EVENTUALLY RETURN TO YOUR WORLD, CORRECT?

THERE'S NO REASON FOR YOU TO KNOW EVERYTHING ABOUT THIS PLACE.

LET SLEEPING DOGS LIE.

Yikes.

Y-YOU SURE DO KNOW SOME WEIRD PEOPLE, HUH?

His mask's all... bloody.

UH-- DO YOU KNOW THAT GUY, JULIUS?

CLACK
CLACK
CLACK
CLACK
CLACK
CLACK

I CAN **SMELL** THE BLOOD ON HIM!

YES.

HEY, ALICE!

IT'S BEEN A WHILE.

WHAT?

HEH HEH.

ALTHOUGH... NOT REALLY, I GUESS.

ACE!

THAT VOICE!

WHAT WAS THAT?

OH, JUST TALKING TO MYSELF!

WHOA. I GUESS JULIUS...

MUMBLE

...REALLY WANTS YOU TO LIKE HIM.

I WANTED TO ASK HIM ABOUT THE BLACK SHADOWS I SAW OUTSIDE AND THE CORPSE! AMONG OTHER THINGS.

• • • • • • • •

RIGHT.

THEY'RE CALLED "AFTERIMAGES."

NOT TO CHANGE THE SUBJECT.

AFTER-IMAGES...

...BUT YOU KNOW THOSE BLACK SHADOWS YOU SAW?

AFTERIMAGES DON'T HAVE PHYSICAL BODIES.

THEN... ARE THEY GHOSTS?!

"I HAVE TO CLEAN THIS UP BEFORE THE AFTERIMAGES APPEAR."

Heh heh.

NO-- THEY'RE NOT GHOSTS.

THEY'RE JUST THINGS THAT EXIST AS A MATTER OF FACT HERE.

HEH.

WELL...

SORRY-- THAT'S ALL I CAN TELL YOU.

THEN WHAT ABOUT THE CLOCK THE SHADOWS TOOK AWAY WITH THEM?

THE SOLDIER AT THE CASTLE MENTIONED SOMETHING ABOUT THAT.

I HAVE TO KEEP IT SECRET OR JULIUS WILL GET UPSET.

Shh.

YOU TWO SOUND CLOSE.

SO I CAN'T TELL YOU ABOUT THE SHADOWS...

...OR MY WORK, ALL RIGHT?

EVEN AMONG THE "ONES WITH DUTIES," I LIKE HIM A LOT.

YEAH, WE ARE.

AFTER ALL, I'M HIS FRIEND.

ONES WITH DUTIES.

NIGHTMARE.

AND YOU SAW WHAT THEY DO.

YOU SAW AN AFTERIMAGE, DIDN'T YOU?

THE CORPSES OF THE INHABITANTS OF THIS WORLD CAN'T KEEP THEIR FORM. ONLY CLOCKS ARE LEFT BEHIND...AND THE AFTERIMAGES CLEAN THEM UP.

♥5 In the Amusement Park

UM...

...YIKES.

SINCE THEY'RE AT WAR WITH THE MAFIA AND THE CASTLE, I THOUGHT THE PARK WOULD BE A LITTLE MORE...SAVAGE.

"NOT SPARKLY."

THIS PLACE IS RIGHT OUT OF A FAIRY TALE AGAIN.

MY HEAD IS FULL OF THE LAMEST FANTASIES.

?

REALLY? I THOUGHT ALL AMUSEMENT PARKS WERE LIKE THIS.

GOOD AFTERNOON!

SCREECH
SCREECH
SCREECH
SQUA
SQUA
SQUA
SQUEE
NO!
LA LA LAA
LA LAA LA
LA LAA!
NOOOOOO!

GOWLAND!

IS HE IN A BETTER MOOD ALREADY?

THAT'S WEIRD.

MAKE YOURSELF COMFORT-ABLE, HATTER.

SORRY TO PUT YOU THROUGH THE TROUBLE OF COMING ALL THE WAY OUT HERE!

GRIIIN

WELL, IF IT ISN'T *HATTER.* LONG TIME NO SEE.

SO YOU CAME TO NEGOTIATE TERRITORIES, DID YA?

HEH HEH!

YOU'VE GOT SOME BALLS IF A BULLET DOESN'T EVEN MAKE YOU FLINCH.

BUT NOW I'M REALLY MAD!

...I CAN'T BELIEVE HE SHOT THE HAT.

Blood!

CLICK

ALTHOUGH I GUESS THIS WAS GONNA HAPPEN EVENTUALLY.

BOSS!

LADY!

THERE THEY ARE, THERE THEY ARE!

HELLOOOO!

LOOKS LIKE THE OWNER CALMED DOWN AFTER HE WENT ALL NUTSY.

BUT HE MIGHT GET MAD AGAIN IF HE SEES YOU, BOSS.

You said some pretty mean stuff to him.

AS IF NOTHING HAPPENED.

I...didn't notice.

Nice day today! Isn't it, Boris?

WHAT HAPPENED WITH GOW-LAND?

IS THAT SO?

I SUPPOSE I'LL HAVE TO GO BACK AND DISCUSS THINGS WITH HIM LATER, THEN.

BOSS, YOU'RE OKAY!

YES.

THIS IS SUPPOSED TO BE A WORLD WHERE EVERYONE WILL FALL IN LOVE WITH ME.

I'M NOT SURE I BELIEVE THAT, ACTUALLY.

...HE DOESN'T DISLIKE ME, RIGHT? THAT WAS ATTRACTION? I THINK?

BUT IF WHAT BLOOD SAID EARLIER WAS TRUE...

YOU SURE FLIRT WITH ALICE A LOT.

HEY, BLOOD.

DO YOU ACTUALLY LIKE HER? I MEAN, FOR REAL?

AND I'D LIKE TO HAVE AN OUTSIDER, SOMEONE UNUSUAL, ON MY ARM.

I'M INTERESTED IN HER.

IF I GET BORED OF HER, I CAN JUST KILL HER.

NOW COME, ELLIOT-- MY HOT TEA AWAITS.

Alice in the Country of Hearts ~
Wonderful Wonder World~ 1 The End

In the next volume of...

Alice IN THE COUNTRY OF Hearts

As Alice grows accustomed to life in Wonderland, she begins to understand the inner workings of this mysterious world. As everyone desires to get close to her, Alice's life lights up with little moments of happiness. However, along with those sweet moments, she soon discovers the truth behind all the bliss…and wasted lives. And what is Alice's reaction when the greatest secret is revealed by Julius, the one and only clock repairer?!